THIS BOOK BELONGS TO:

_____

THE WONDERFUL WORLD OF BEARDED DRAGONS

Mimi Jones

Dedicated to all who love the beardies.

ISBN 978-1-958985-83-0

www.joeysavestheday.com

A Mimi Book

Bearded dragons are reptiles from Australia, known for their calm nature and friendly personalities.

Their name comes from the spiky "beard" under their chin, which they can puff out when needed. They puff out their beard to look bigger, especially when they feel excited, nervous, or curious.

There are eight different species of bearded dragons, each with its own unique traits.

UNIQUE

They are one of the most popular pet reptiles because they are easy to care for and handle. Bearded dragons are gentle creatures that usually enjoy being held and spending time with people.

Their mouths naturally curve upward, giving them a friendly, smiling appearance.

They are diurnal, which means they are awake during the day and sleep at night like humans.

Diurnal

Nocturnal

Adult bearded dragons can grow up to 18–22 inches long from head to tail.

18 — 22

Bearded dragons come from the dry deserts and warm forests of Australia.

Australia

They live in scrublands, savannas, and woodlands where the sun shines brightly.

Scrublands

Savanas

Woodlands

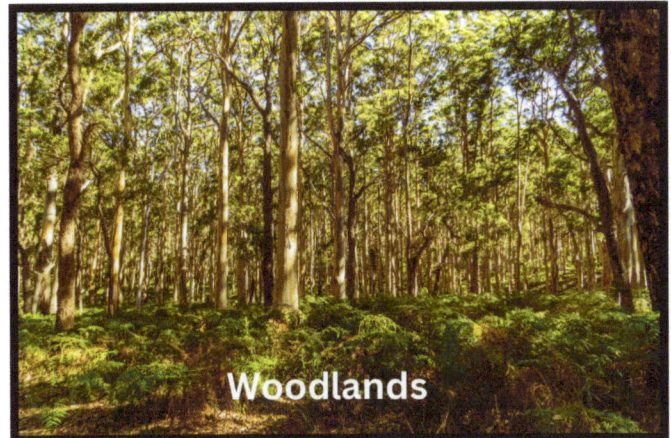

They climb trees and branches to look for food and to get a better view of their surroundings.

NATURAL

Their natural colors help them blend into sandy or rocky environments for protection.

They are most active in the early morning and late afternoon when temperatures are comfortable.

PROTECT

Their bodies are covered in tough, spiky scales that help protect them from danger.

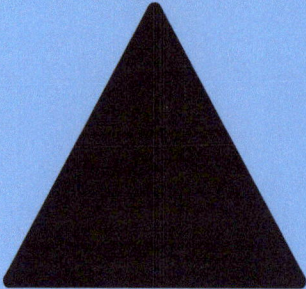

TRIANGLE

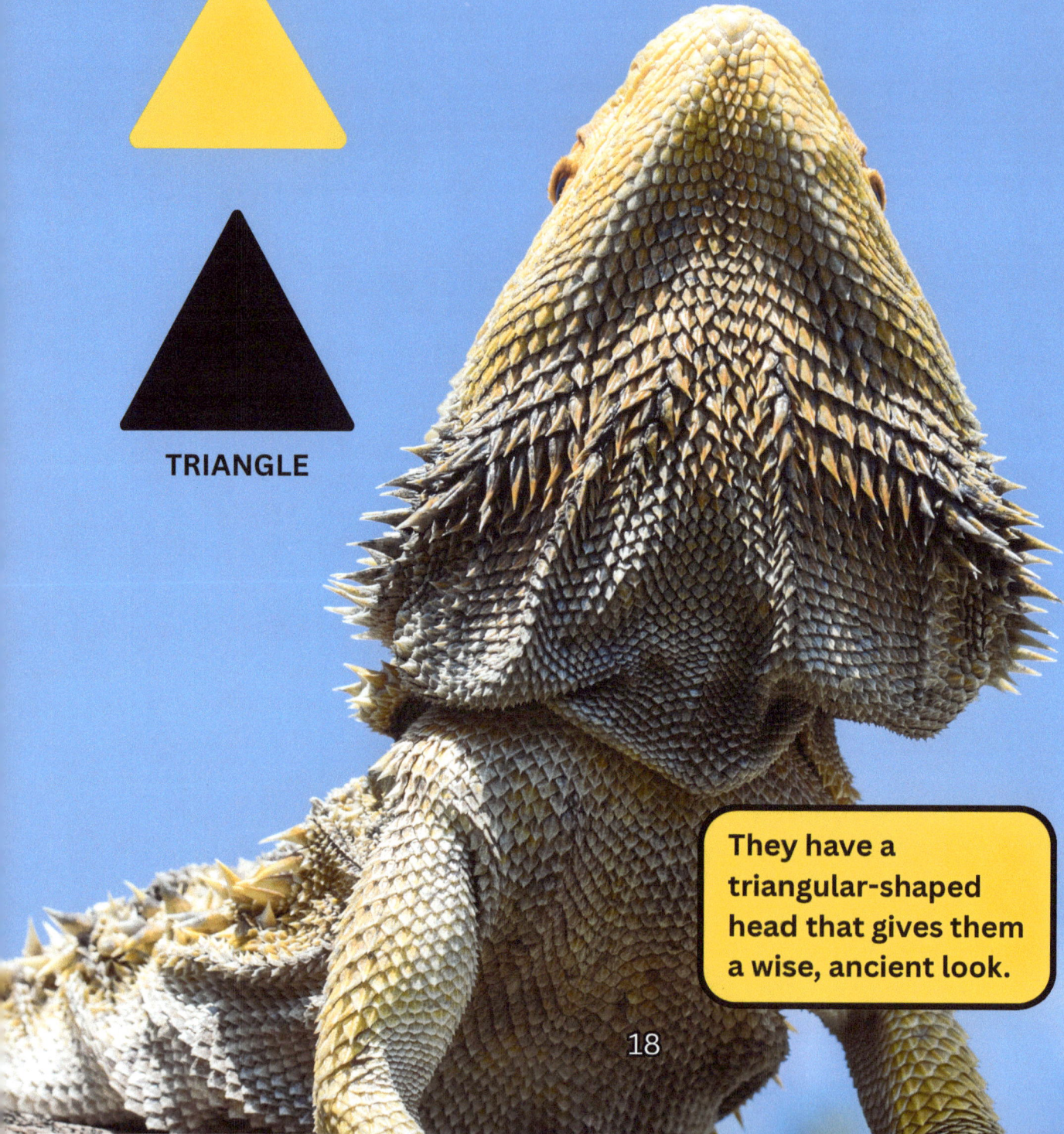

They have a triangular-shaped head that gives them a wise, ancient look.

Their strong legs help them climb rocks, branches, and other surfaces with ease.

STRONG!

Their long tails help them balance and make up almost half their total length.

½

BALANCE

The third eye is in this area.

They have a "third eye" on top of their head that senses light and shadows.

They have excellent vision and can see colors even better than humans.

They can run on their hind legs when startled, which makes them look like tiny dinosaurs.

They enjoy climbing and exploring new objects in their environment.

They open their mouths while basking to release extra heat, a behavior called "gaping."

Bearded dragons are omnivores, meaning they eat both plants and insects to stay healthy.

Dandelion Greens

Dubia Roach

They enjoy insects like crickets, roaches, and worms as part of their diet.

Cricket

Roach

Worm

They use their sticky tongues to catch insects quickly and accurately.

In the wild, they drink water droplets from leaves or morning dew.

wild

CARE

Bearded dragons usually live 4–10 years, depending on their care and environment.

With excellent care, some bearded dragons can live even longer than average.

Female bearded dragons lay clutches of eggs in sandy nests that they dig themselves.

Baby dragons are tiny when they hatch, only a few inches long. They grow very quickly during their first year of life.

Bearded dragons can sleep standing up, which makes them look like tiny statues.

They tilt their heads when curious, almost like they're trying to understand something.

Their long claws help them grip branches and dig into the ground.

Count the bearded dragons.

Thank you for exploring the fun and fascinating world of bearded dragons with us! We hope you had as much fun as a bearded dragon soaking up the sunshine on a warm rock. If this book made you smile or taught you something new, feel free to share it with a friend and leave a little review. Your support helps more curious kids discover these amazing reptiles.

Check out these other interesting books in the
Wonderful World of series!

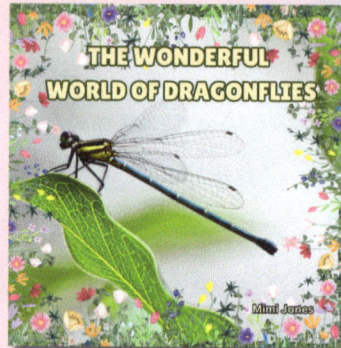

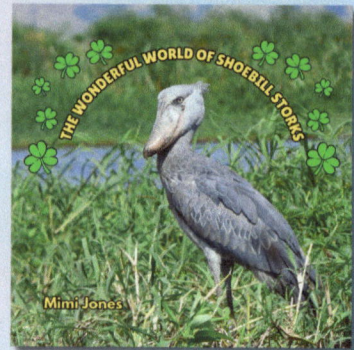

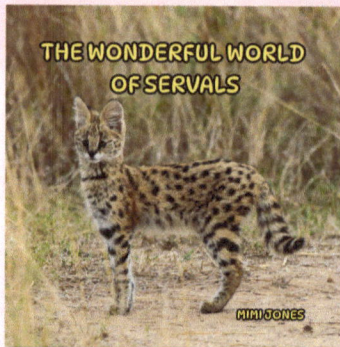

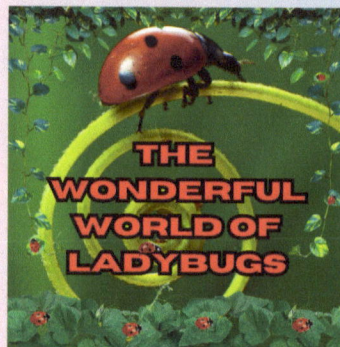

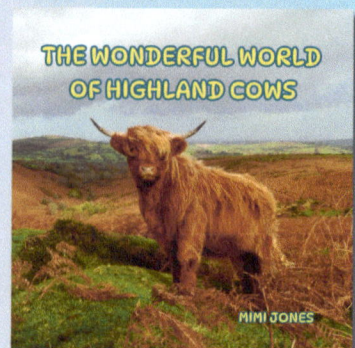

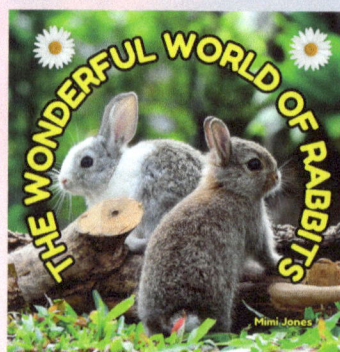

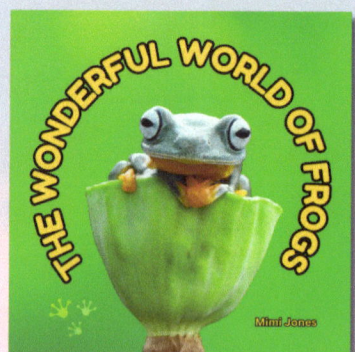

THE WONDERFUL WORLD OF SUNFLOWERS

THE WONDERFUL WORLD OF DRAGONFLIES
Mimi Jones

THE WONDERFUL WORLD OF SHOEBILL STORKS
Mimi Jones

THE WONDERFUL WORLD OF SERVALS
MIMI JONES

THE WONDERFUL WORLD OF LADYBUGS

THE WONDERFUL WORLD OF HIGHLAND COWS
MIMI JONES

THE WONDERFUL WORLD OF PANDAS
Mimi Jones

THE WONDERFUL WORLD OF RABBITS
Mimi Jones

THE WONDERFUL WORLD OF FROGS
Mimi Jones

www.mimibooks.com

www.ingramcontent.com/pod-product-compliance
Lightning Source LLC
Chambersburg PA
CBHW041548040426
42447CB00002B/91